SCHOLASTIC

Let's Find Out

My REBUS Reader

I0890041

Fire Safety Pups!

by Vivian Basset

SCHOLASTIC INC.

New York Toronto London Auckland Sydney New Delhi Hong Kong

Is it safe to touch a  ? **Yes.**

flower

Is it safe to touch  matches? **No.**

Is it safe to touch a  ? **Yes.**

shoe

Is it safe to touch a hot  ? **No.**

pot

Is it safe to touch a  ? **Yes.**

ball

Is it safe to touch a  ? **No.**

candle

Which of these are safe to touch?

Which of these are not safe to touch?